Act Love Walk

A 4-WEEK STUDENT DISCIPLESHIP JOURNAL

THIS BOOK BELONGS TO:

Anna V.

LeaderTreks

Making Disciples...Developing Leaders

Act.Love.Walk: A 4-Week Student Discipleship Journal
© 2015 by LeaderTreks. All rights reserved.

ISBN: 978-1-939031-27-3

Published by LeaderTreks
25W560 Geneva Road, Suite 30
Carol Stream, IL 60188

www.leadertreks.com
877-502-0699

CONTENTS

Missing the Point

Has a friend ever completely let you down? Maybe they gossiped about you or deserted you to hang out with someone else. It's the worst. And when (or if) they finally come to their senses and start to feel bad, they try to make it up to you in all sorts of ways: by showering you with attention, saving you a spot at lunch, or buying you coffee. While these things are nice, what you really wanted in the first place wasn't a free cup of coffee; you wanted a trustworthy friend.

In the book of Micah, this same scenario happened between God and the people who said they loved him. They abandoned him and rebelled against him. Then, in a desperate attempt to make it up to him, the people tried all sorts of sacrifices and rituals to make it up to God. But they completely missed the point. What God really wanted wasn't their last-minute, feel-bad sacrifices; he wanted their hearts. So God sent Micah to get that message to them, to bring them back to the basics of how to follow God. The highlight of Micah's message is the following verse:

"HE HAS SHOWED YOU, O MAN, WHAT IS GOOD. AND WHAT DOES THE LORD REQUIRE OF YOU? TO ACT JUSTLY AND TO LOVE MERCY AND TO WALK HUMBLY WITH YOUR GOD" (MICAH 6:8).

Over the next several weeks, we're going to take a look at what it really means to act justly, to love mercy, and to walk humbly with God. Not in a make-it-up-to-God kind of way, but in a give-our-hearts-to-God kind of way.

SO LET'S GET STARTED.

How It Works

This book includes four weeks of journal pages to challenge the way you understand God's expectations. Each week takes you through six days of questions to get you thinking, Bible studies to shift your perspective, and challenges to stretch you out of your comfort zone. Then, on the seventh day of the week, you'll get a break to recharge for the next section. It'll help you get into a rhythm of learning, growing, and putting that knowledge into action.

Throughout this journal, you'll also find the MARKS OF A DISCIPLE. These are things that Christ-followers are committed to and have in common, like connecting with God through prayer, applying his Word to our lives, serving without personal agendas, managing God's gifts, and many other things.

Marks Of A Disciple

Remember, you'll get out of this book what you put into it. The challenges you'll encounter won't always be easy—they're designed to stretch you! Take a risk and do your best to engage each day with energy and passion. When we make ourselves available to God, he'll transform us and use us in ways that will blow our minds!

x x x x x x x x x x x x x x x x x x x x x x x x x x x x x x x x

WEEK ONE

act justly

DAY ONE *intro*

✕ ✕

HE HAS SHOWED YOU, O MAN, WHAT IS GOOD. AND WHAT DOES THE LORD REQUIRE OF YOU? TO *ACT JUSTLY* AND TO LOVE MERCY AND TO WALK HUMBLY WITH YOUR GOD. MICAH 6:8

Why do we have laws, police officers, and judges? Injustice. It is a cause of suffering around the world and the basis for countless wars throughout history. Something inside of us wants life to be fair. We want to world to be just. That's why even small children get upset when somebody cuts in line. That's the reason sports fans yell at referees when they don't agree with their calls. That's the foundation for many professions in our justice system: lawyers, social workers, police officers, soldiers, doctors, and even politicians.

We expect police officers to act justly—it's their job! But what does it mean to act justly when it's not what you're paid to do? When God spoke through the prophet Micah and told his people to "act justly," what did he mean? What does it look like to act justly while still navigating life as a teenager?

These are some of the questions we'll try to answer this week as we go deeper into Micah's words from God.

DAY ONE
justice, big and small

Acting justly is the first of three expectations God brought up to his people when they got lazy in their faith. These people were really good at saying the right things and justifying the wrong things. But they were missing the point. So God used Micah to intervene and get them back on track.

It's easy to think big when it comes to justice. From the fight against human trafficking to racial reconciliation, the word *justice* can bring to mind some pretty big issues that seem out of our control. But when Micah says that God wants us to act justly, he isn't only talking about sometime down the road when you're able to face giant global issues.

He's talking about doing the right thing here and now, when it's small and no one will see, when it's uncomfortable, and when it doesn't feel worth it. Because when we act justly in our daily lives and decisions, we are preparing ourselves to fight for the kind of justice that intervenes in world hunger, corrupt systems, human trafficking, and more.

SPEND A FEW MINUTES TODAY ANSWERING THESE QUESTIONS ABOUT JUSTICE AND YOUR OWN LIFE.

If you could change one tragic event in the history of the world, what would you change and why?

I wouldnt change anything. The past events that happned in world history are what shapes us as humans. But if I were to cheese, probably the equality

Pretend you are the President of the United States. What is the first law you would try to change? Who is the first person you would try to help?

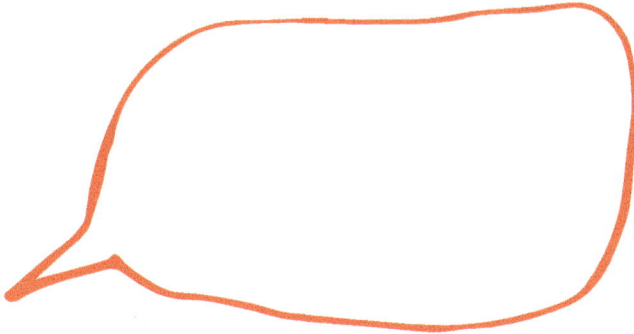

Have you ever had to help two friends resolve a dispute? yes
How did you decide who was right and who was wrong?

In my situation, I listered to both sides of therye stories and cheose to let both of them go Even thogh it was hard, I think it was a goode desicion

How do you identify injustices around you?

What's the difference between justice and revenge?

DAY TWO
stopping and starting

Israel was known as God's nation. But although they said they were following him, they often weren't (just like a lot of us). So God sent prophets like Micah to speak God's words to Israel and get them back on track.

Another of these prophets God sent was Isaiah. Sometimes Isaiah rebuked God's people, sometimes he reminded them of what God had done for them in the past, and sometimes he provided guidance for what they needed to start doing. That guidance came in two different types of commands: stop doing something or start doing something else. Isaiah 1:16–23 is a passage that gives both of these commands.

USE THE 5P BIBLE STUDY METHOD TO STUDY ISAIAH 1:16-23 FOR YOURSELF.

PURPOSE Why do you think the author wrote this? Why is it important enough to be in the Bible? In a sentence or two, write what you think the overall theme or topic is.

>>>

PRIMARY VERSE Which verse or phrase stands out to you the most? What do you think is catching your attention?

>>>

PROMISES List any promises you find. You may need to think deeply about this one because promises are sometimes inferred or implied.

>>>

PROBLEMS If you read something here that doesn't make sense to you—a word, a phrase, an idea—write it down as a question. Then search for the answer by asking someone who might understand the Bible a bit better.

>>>

PRACTICAL APPLICATION Think about how this passage might actually change your life. What needs to be different in how you live, think, and feel? Be specific—your application should tell who, what, and when.

>>>

DAY THREE
influence

//

Tony was born with cerebral palsy, but he didn't let it stop him from achieving his goals. He graduated from high school and was accepted to a prestigious university. Unfortunately the campus was large and spread out, so some of Tony's classes were a bit of trek, especially since he used a walker to get from one place to another.

It took Tony up to an hour and half to get from one class to the next. Some days Tony skipped lunch because he didn't have time to eat if he wanted to make it to class on time.

Taylor was another a student at Tony's university. He saw Tony's struggle and approached the school about doing something to help students like Tony move around campus. Getting no response, Taylor took matters into his own hands. He set up a GoFundMe page to raise money so he could buy Tony a mobility scooter. With the help of his friends, Taylor raised more than enough money and presented the scooter to a grateful Tony, who can now zip around campus.

Sometimes justice looks like fighting to change laws and save lives. Other times it looks like giving something to someone in need and using your influence and power to make a godly change.

PICK ONE (OR MORE) OF THE FOLLOWING CHALLENGES TO DO IN THE NEXT 24 HOURS, AND WRITE ABOUT YOUR EXPERIENCE.

>> Apologize to someone you once bullied. You may not have even realized you were doing it at the time. Maybe you made a joke at someone's expense or left someone out of something.

>> Combat prejudice by inviting somebody who looks different to join you for lunch. Spend the time getting to know them as an individual rather than a stereotype.

>> Scroll through your social media history. What have you posted or reposted that had something to do with awareness about an injustice. Choose one injustice and move from simply posting about it to taking action in the next 24 hours. Do any of the following: Pray for the people involved. Learn about and volunteer at an organization that helps in this area. Donate money or spend some time asking questions and getting to know someone who has been affected by this injustice.

>> Find 10 different organizations in your community that work to fight injustice. Make a list of the organizations, the people they serve, and the needs they have.

>> Do a Google News search for "humanitarian crisis." Read at least three articles about one crisis. Then research ways you could help.

What was hard about this?

What did you learn?

Did anything surprise you?

DAY FOUR
power

× ×

You've probably heard the story of Oscar Schindler, whose life was depicted in the movie *Schindler's List*. Oscar was a Nazi—a spy actually—during World War 2. He ran an enamelware factory, and his life goal was to make a lot of money. One of the best ways to make money during WW2 was to hire Jews, since they were considered worthless and could be paid less than anyone else. So Schindler's factory grew in its number of Jewish workers.

It didn't take long before Schindler's power grew immensely. His factory was considered vital to the war effort, which gave him a lot of business. As a member of the Nazi party, he knew the inside information on decisions before most people. He learned that a ghetto was about to be cleared out and all Jews sent to extermination or concentration camps, so he had his workers stay in the factory overnight in order to keep his work force. But witnessing the clearing of the ghetto changed Schindler's heart and his goals.

From this point on, Schindler used his power and influence to save Jews. He used every connection he had with high-ranking Nazis to pay bribes that would keep his workers safe. He built safe housing for them, and even changed his whole business from cookware to anti-tank grenades so the Nazis would consider it vital and not shut it down. In the end, Schindler acted justly by tapping out his bank account, using all his persuasive power, and wielding his influence to save Jewish people.

As a student, you may feel completely powerless. You might not feel like you have any influence at all. You're also pretty far from desperate situations like the Holocaust of WW2. But take a step back and really consider what power and influence you do have. How can you use it to act justly?

MAKE A LIST OF ALL THE AREAS IN YOUR LIFE WHERE YOU HAVE INFLUENCE OR POWER.

NEXT TO EACH ITEM, WRITE DOWN WHAT IT WOULD LOOK LIKE TO ACT JUSTLY USING THAT INFLUENCE OR POWER.

Marks Of A Disciple

DISCIPLES OF CHRIST USE THEIR *INFLUENCE* AND *POWER* TO PROMOTE GOD'S JUSTICE. (ISAIAH 1:17)

What kind of influence does social media or the Internet give you?

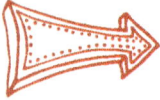

When you spend money, how are you wielding influence or power?

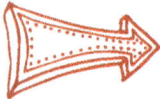

How do your words give you influence and power?

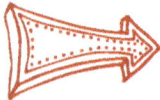

How do you get influence and power from the way you spend your time?

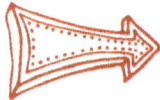

Now take a look at all the answers you've written down, and think of one thing you can do in the next 24 hours to act justly with your influence. Be specific. Maybe it's looking into the companies you frequently buy from to see how they treat their workers. Or maybe it's using your words to support someone who is struggling and needs encouragement.

"JUSTICE IS THE GRAMMAR OF THINGS. MERCY IS THE POETRY OF THINGS."

–

FREDRICK BUECHNER

DAY FIVE
imitating God

In the beginning of Ephesians 5, Paul tells the Christ-followers in a city called Ephesus to imitate God like children imitate their parents. Children watch their parents closely. Little boys want to shave like Daddy. Little girls try on Mom's makeup. These imitations are their attempts to be like the people they love and respect. If we are going to imitate God, our heavenly Father, then we must see the world the way he does and respond to things as he would. Part of that means we should act justly, choosing to do the right thing regardless of the circumstances.

TAKE SOME TIME TO STUDY EPHESIANS 5:1–11, USING THE SPECK BIBLE STUDY METHOD.

SINS TO AVOID

Make a list of any sins—wrong actions, attitudes, or thoughts—mentioned in the passage. These are the things to avoid in your life.

PROMISES TO CLAIM

Make a list of the promises in this passage. Promises give us confidence when we doubt God or face difficult times. So take them to heart and believe what they say.

EXAMPLES TO FOLLOW

What examples do you find in the passage? Is there a right way of thinking or acting described in the passage that you should take as an example for your life? Write it down.

COMMANDS TO OBEY

Write out all the commands you find. If a passage encourages you to take a certain action, take it as a command and write it down.

KNOWLEDGE OF GOD TO APPLY

What does the passage tell you about God that you can apply to your daily life? God's character shines throughout the Bible as an example for us.

DAY SIX
assumptions

//

Injustice happens when people view one another differently than God does, when we refuse to acknowledge that every person who has ever walked or will ever walk on this planet was created in the image of God. Sometimes we look at things in this world and jump to conclusions. We believe stereotypes instead of learning the facts about an individual. Sadly, this just fuels injustice.

To act justly means to see people as God does. In all likelihood, that means you'll have to change the way you think about some things (Rom. 12:2). Are you up for that challenge?

Consider the following crises. What do you know about these situations? What do you assume about the people involved? How do you think God views the people suffering these injustices? How does your thinking need to change in order for you to act justly?

Spend some time filling in the chart below and journaling your thoughts about each injustice. Take the challenge a step further by learning more about specific individuals who fought against each of these injustices. The first row is already filled in as an example for you.

INJUSTICE	ASSUMPTIONS (What are some assumptions people make about this injustice that may or may not be true?)	THE FACTS (Do a Google search to find some facts you didn't already know. Try to use only reliable sources.)	GOD'S VIEW (How does God see the situation and the people involved?)
PROSTITUTION	Some people sell their bodies so others can have sex with them. They chose this life. They need the money.	Some prostitutes are trafficked humans who are enslaved by oppressors. Some were abused as children.	These women are sinners in need of a Savior. They are people, not objects

INJUSTICE	ASSUMPTIONS	THE FACTS	GOD'S VIEW
RACISM			
HOMELESSNESS			
CHILD LABOR			
ABUSE			
REFUGEES			
ABORTION			

What are three surprising things you learned about these injustices from your research?

Were any of your original assumptions incorrect?

What are a few things you can do based on the information you learned?

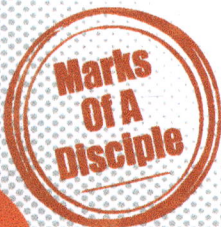

Marks Of A Disciple

DISCIPLES OF CHRIST *ACT JUSTLY.*
(PSALM 106:3)

"THERE MAY BE TIMES WHEN WE ARE POWERLESS TO PREVENT INJUSTICE, BUT THERE MUST NEVER BE A TIME WHEN WE FAIL TO PROTEST."

–

**ELIE WIESEL
FROM HIS NOBEL LECTURE**

DAY SEVEN
Sabbath

//

Have you ever heard someone refer to Sunday as the Sabbath? That means it's our day of rest. Even though we usually think of Sunday as our Sabbath day, Sabbath was originally celebrated on Saturday, the last day of the week. Jewish people still observe their day of rest on Saturday, calling it "Shabbat." Sabbath originated in Genesis when God rested on the seventh day of creation.

So today, on the last day of this week in your journal, that's your challenge. Rest! Reflect on what you've learned so far, the challenges you did, or Bible verses that stuck out to you. Spend some time praying and talking with God. Recharge your batteries and refresh your mind. Then come back tomorrow ready to dig into what it means to love mercy.

"BY THE SEVENTH DAY GOD HAD FINISHED THE WORK HE HAD BEEN DOING; SO ON THE SEVENTH DAY HE RESTED FROM ALL HIS WORK." –GENESIS 2:2

"INJUSTICE ANYWHERE IS A THREAT TO JUSTICE EVERYWHERE."

–

MARTIN LUTHER KING, JR., LETTER FROM BIRMINGHAM JAIL

WEEK TWO

love mercy

DAY ONE *intro*

x x x x x x x x x x x x x x x x x x x x x x x

HE HAS SHOWED YOU, O MAN, WHAT IS GOOD. AND WHAT DOES THE LORD REQUIRE OF YOU? TO ACT JUSTLY AND TO *LOVE MERCY* AND TO WALK HUMBLY WITH YOUR GOD.
MICAH 6:8

It's a good thing for us that God isn't only just, but he's also merciful. Justice alone means looking at humanity and saying, "That's broken and sinful." Sin leads to death and separation from God. That's justice—pretty bleak, isn't it?

But God is also merciful. He saw our sin and made a way for us to be reunited with him again. God's mercy doesn't undermine his justice. In a completely unique way, his mercy makes his justice even more just! God's justice and mercy were displayed on the Cross. He pointed at sin and said, "That's not right! It needs to be destroyed." But instead of wiping out all sinners, Jesus took the penalty of sin—death—on himself so justice would reign and our relationship with him would remain. When we act justly, we reflect God's character. But we're missing something essential if we don't also love mercy.

This week we're digging into why it's so important to love mercy. Through journaling, Bible study, and prayer, you will explore what it means to receive mercy from God, rest in that mercy, and then share that mercy with others in your life.

DAY ONE
Lord have mercy

//

We don't really *do* mercy today. We live in a culture with a hair trigger when it comes to outrage. One wrong tweet, a single careless remark, or a simple mistake can make someone an outsider, unemployable, or even a criminal. And in the age of the Internet, everything everyone says and does is scrutinized—even a misinterpreted joke can lead to public and unrelenting condemnation.

Mercy isn't our strong suit. So it's little surprise that the word mercy doesn't make its way into our lives very often. But mercy is actually central to being a Christ-follower. Jesus himself taught us that a sinner pleading, "Lord have mercy on me a sinner," was more holy than any religious leader's most sophisticated and wordy prayer.

> **BEGIN TODAY BY REFLECTING ON MERCY'S PLACE IN YOUR LIFE AND FAITH:**

When and where do you hear the word *mercy* in daily life?

Without reading ahead (or Googling anything), how would you define the word *mercy*?

Why would mercy be such a key piece of a Christ-follower's life?

How often do you ask God for mercy? What might be different about your life if you focused on God's mercy more often?

On a scale of 1 to 5 (with 1 being very low and 5 being very high) how merciful do you think you are? Why do you give yourself that rating?

Where in the world around you do you see the greatest need for more mercy? Where in your school? Where in your church?

DAY TWO
right reactions

Before we begin today, try to imagine the sound of air escaping from a large balloon.

We've all been that balloon—pumped full of pride and righteous anger. We know that we're right. We feel proud, big, confident, and bold. We love that feeling when we know in our gut that we are on the right side of something big.

And then it happens. Just as we are celebrating how right we are and how wrong someone else is, we get put in our place. A friend points out that we aren't actually right. A Google search finds a fact that proves us wrong, or someone wiser and more mature tells us that we're making a big deal out of nothing. Our self-righteousness slips out of us faster than the air from a balloon, and there is nowhere remote enough for us to hide. That moment of deflation is powerful!

If you imagine the last time you felt that way, you might be able to feel what it was like to be one of the men you're about to read about who caught a woman in adultery. They came to Jesus, puffed up with righteous anger, with the law on their side. But check out how Jesus responded to these over-inflated balloons.

TODAY WE MOVE FROM TALKING ABOUT THE CONCEPT OF MERCY TO SEEING IT PERFECTLY ENACTED BY JESUS. USE THE OPA METHOD TO STUDY THIS FROM JOHN 8:1–11.

OBSERVATION

Compile all the facts found in these passages. Make 20 to 30 observations about what you read.

>>

PRINCIPLES

Draw a few principles from the observations you made. What is God trying to teach you in this passage?

>>

APPLICATION

How will you apply these principles to your life? Be specific—a good application will tell who, what, and when.

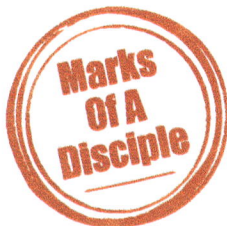

>>

Marks Of A Disciple

DISCIPLES OF CHRIST *LOVE MERCY*. (LUKE 6:36)

DAY THREE
mercy challenge

//

Think of a person or a group that you hold in low regard—a person or group that you, in particular, struggle to love and appreciate.

WRITE YOUR PERSON OR GROUP HERE: _____

First, consider: Why do you feel this way? Is your feeling rooted in pride or selfishness? Is it because they are lower than you in social standing? Or maybe because of something they do or have done that genuinely makes them worthy of your anger?

WRITE DOWN, HONESTLY, WHY YOU STRUGGLE TO LOVE THIS GROUP OR PERSON:

Now, consider this: God created them, loves them, and desires to be in relationship with them just as he does with you. Read the words of Jonah in Jonah 4. Do Jonah's words sound like something you'd say?

Now, re-read Jonah 4:11. If God were to respond to you about the person or group you are struggling to love, what might he say?

WRITE HERE WHAT GOD MIGHT SAY:

When it comes to mercy, seeing our enemies through the eyes of God is only half of the battle. We also have to work to re-learn our responses to those people. Taking meaningful, loving action toward those we hate, resent, or disrespect has the power to change our hearts. Pick one of the following powerful ways to change your thoughts and behavior. Then do it!

Pray every day this week for the person or group you struggle with to receive God's full blessing in their lives.

Go to someone to whom you've complained about another person and apologize for gossiping. Explain that you were wrong and ask them to call you out if you start to tear down another person or group around them again.

Do something kind for the person or group you struggle with.

If you dislike this person (or group) from a distance, take a step to spend time with that person or a person from that group.

Which action will you take this week and when will you take it?

DAY FOUR
you need mercy

A recent study was done in which people were shown a video of a car driving recklessly fast down an interstate. The people in the study were asked to evaluate the video and draw conclusions about the driver. Most participants described the driver as careless, thoughtless, and selfish. They saw someone being cruel and anti-social. They imagined the driver as only operating from bad motives.

Then the researchers showed the video to participants and asked them to imagine themselves as the driver. "Why would you be driving like this?" they asked. Suddenly the answers changed. Very few described themselves in the situation as careless, thoughtless, or selfish. Most imagined themselves as responding to a medical emergency or another kind of crisis. They could see a lot of good reasons for taking an action that was dangerous when they imagined themselves in that seat.

The truth is that judgment without mercy is built into our sinful human nature. We see our own actions (even when they are dangerous or just plain wrong) with mercy, but too rarely extend that to others. That's what's reflected in this powerful quote from Thomas Adams, the inventor of chewing gum (cool, right?).

"HE THAT DEMANDS MERCY AND SHOWS NONE RUINS THE BRIDGE OVER WHICH HE HIMSELF IS TO PASS."
-THOMAS ADAMS

Spend some time reflecting on mercy in your own life by answering these questions.

Why is showing mercy so closely tied to receiving mercy?

Why is it so easy to ask for mercy but so hard to give it?

When's the last time you had a "speeding car" moment? When have you judged someone for their actions before you knew the full story?

Have you ever forgiven someone else and benefited from them being merciful to you later?

What stories or passages from Scripture can you think of that reflect Adams's quote?

DAY FIVE
get it, give it

Have you ever noticed that as soon as a new iPhone comes out, the early adopters cannot wait to show it to everyone in their lives. "Look at this!" they say to anyone within earshot. "Did you know it does this now?" they ask, hoping you will be astounded by the new features.

These Apple owners' reactions show us a profound truth about the things we own: we only experience the full joy of a gift or possession when we share it with others. C.S. Lewis (who wrote way before there were smart phones to brag about) said it this way: "Nothing that you have not given away will ever be really yours." But Lewis didn't write that about a physical possession—he wrote it about the gospel.

Everyone who gets an iPhone enthusiastically shows it to their friends. And when we experience the life-changing mercy of Jesus, we should be compelled to share it freely in the same way. The problem of merciless Christians is not that they simply fail to show mercy; it's that they likely have never truly experienced it themselves.

TODAY YOU'LL READ FROM A LETTER WRITTEN BY PAUL (AN EXPERT ON GOD'S MERCY) THAT SHOULD SERVE AS A REFRESHER ON THE GOSPEL AS A POWERFUL MESSAGE OF MERCY. USE THE 5P METHOD TO STUDY TITUS 3:4-8 AND REFLECT ON WHETHER YOU'VE TRULY OWNED AND SHARED THE POWERFUL TRUTH THIS PASSAGE COMMUNICATES.

PURPOSE Why do you think the author wrote this? Why is it important enough to be in the Bible? In a sentence or two, write what you think the overall theme or topic is.

PRIMARY VERSE Which verse or phrase stands out to you the most? What do you think is catching your attention?

PROMISES List any promises you find. You may need to think deeply about this one because promises are sometimes inferred or implied.

PROBLEMS If you read something here that doesn't make sense to you—a word, a phrase, an idea—write it down as a question. Then search for the answer by asking someone who might understand the Bible a bit better.

PRACTICAL APPLICATION Think about how this passage might actually change your life. What needs to be different in how you live, think, and feel? Be specific—your application should tell who, what, and when.

DAY SIX
the mercy effect

Pope Francis' first visit to America was remarkable for a number of reasons. It was his first visit to North America, he was the first Pope to address congress, and it created three days of very different news coverage. Media outlets typically devoted to covering religion through the lens of political battles—or outright mockery—were sharing pictures of the leader of the Roman Catholic Church stooping to pick up a small child. One after another, talking heads from news programs commented that, regardless of their views of his theology, the Pope just seemed, well, like Jesus.

The Pope's take on any given controversial issue isn't really the point. What struck so many was that in his public appearances he shared mercy and humility. People aren't used to leaders—religious or otherwise—who skip the fancy congressional banquet for lunch at a homeless shelter. Yet that is precisely the call to mercy and humility found throughout the New Testament.

When Christians meet the truths and moral demands of Scripture with the humility, self-sacrifice, and mercy of Jesus, even hardened atheists take note. It has been that way since the earliest days of the church. When Christ-followers boldly proclaimed the gospel, they just as boldly fought poverty in their community (Acts 4:34). The Roman Emperor Julian observed, with disdain, that the early church "has been specially advanced through the loving service rendered to strangers and through their care of the burial of the dead. It is a scandal that there is not a single Jew who is a beggar and that the [Christians] care not only for their own poor but for ours as well; while those who belong to us look in vain for the help we should render them."

A merciful Christ-follower is powerful!

TODAY'S CHALLENGE IS TO TAKE AN INSIGHT YOU'VE HAD FROM THIS WEEK'S STUDY ABOUT MERCY AND TO PUT IT INTO ACTION. MAKE A SIMPLE 15-SECOND VIDEO FOR SOCIAL MEDIA SHARING ONE INSIGHT FROM THIS WEEK.

But be careful! If you talk about mercy, you have to be ready to show it. Telling your friends and family that you mean to live out a merciful faith must mean you plan to do it! But it's not impossible—through the work of Christ and the power of the Spirit, you can walk in mercy!

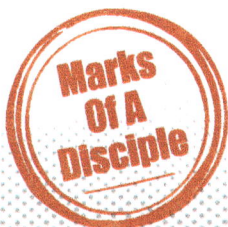

Marks Of A Disciple

DISCIPLES *EMBRACE* THE MERCY THEY'VE RECEIVED FROM CHRIST. (1 PETER 1:3)

DAY SEVEN
relationship

//

"Remember the Sabbath day by keeping it holy. Six days you shall labor and do all your work, but the seventh day is a Sabbath to the Lord your God." –Exodus 20:8–10a

Today, as you take a break from this journal, refocus your thoughts on your relationship with God. Think about how you've seen his mercy in your life, and thank him for it. Reflect on this psalm that talks about the mercy of God. Make it's prayer your own.

"HAVE MERCY ON ME, O GOD, BECAUSE OF YOUR UNFAILING LOVE. BECAUSE OF YOUR GREAT COMPASSION, BLOT OUT THE STAIN OF MY SINS. WASH ME CLEAN FROM MY GUILT. PURIFY ME FROM MY SIN."

-

PSALM 51:1-2

WEEK THREE

walk humbly

DAY ONE *intro*

✗ ✗

HE HAS SHOWED YOU, O MAN, WHAT IS GOOD. AND WHAT DOES THE LORD REQUIRE OF YOU? TO ACT JUSTLY AND TO LOVE MERCY AND TO *WALK HUMBLY WITH YOUR GOD.* MICAH 6:8

Although it's the last thing listed in this verse, the phrase "walk humbly with your God" isn't simply tacked onto the end of Micah 6:8. It's actually the foundation for the things you've learned about so far. In fact, we can't act justly or love mercy if we are not also walking humbly with God. An attitude of humility before God allows us to learn what true justice and mercy look like in our own particular circumstances. It also keeps us from getting prideful as we do the things God asks us to do. Walking humbly reminds us that "all that we have accomplished [God has] done for us" (Isa. 26:12).

But how do we grow in humility? First, we have to know what it is (and humility is difficult to define). It doesn't mean we should always put ourselves down, emphasizing our weaknesses but ignoring our strengths. It isn't avoiding responsibility and always letting others lead. It isn't about groveling or choosing to be disgraced. C.S. Lewis defined humility this way: "Humility is not thinking less of yourself; it is thinking of yourself less." That makes a little more sense, but it's not easy to do—because we think of ourselves a lot!

This week we will look at how we can practice humility in our walk with God, a walk that should be the very foundation of acting justly and loving mercy.

DAY ONE
hunched back pride

//

Imagine going through your day hunched over with your eyes fixed on your own belly button. That's a crazy image, but it's actually how some pretty insightful and well-known theologians (like Augustine and Martin Luther) describe humanity. They coined the term *homo incurvatus in se*, which means "humanity curved in on itself," and they're onto something. Think about it; we walk through our lives looking primarily at ourselves. With every circumstance and person we encounter, we think, "How does this affect me?"

Humility, oddly enough, requires us to pull our eyes away from our bellies to look out toward others and up to God. Pride keeps us hunched over; humility makes us stand tall!

TAKE A FEW MINUTES TO ANSWER THESE QUESTIONS ABOUT HUMILITY IN YOUR OWN LIFE.

Is your tendency to build yourself up or to put yourself down? Why?

How are both of those tendencies examples of being "curved in on yourself"?

Name five ways you see *homo incurvatus in se* affecting your relationships with other people.

- o
- o
- o
- o
- o

If people are walking around focused on themselves, how does this cause injustice and hinder mercy?

How does pride actually make you walk through your day hunched over instead of standing tall? Think through yesterday and list five times you were so focused on yourself that you failed to see the needs of others or didn't hear or obey a prompting from the Holy Spirit to reach out to someone else.

- o
- o
- o
- o
- o

How do you think humility could actually help you walk through life standing up straight?

How could true humility change the ways you look at other people (your friends and family as well as strangers)?

DAY TWO
core beliefs

//

Have you ever heard the phrase "your beliefs inform your actions"? Another way to look at that phrase is by rewording it like this: your actions reveal your beliefs. For instance, if I saw you scrape a bunch of uneaten food into the drain of your sink, I would assume that you believe your garbage disposal will work to grind up the food. You don't doubt its ability to handle the food. I can even assume you've dumped food down the drain many times before and it's never failed. If you flipped the garbage disposal switch and nothing happened, you'd probably stop putting solid food down the drain. Your belief in the garbage disposal's ability informs where you dump your scraps, and your putting food down the drain reveals your firm belief in the garbage disposal.

Read today's verses with that idea in mind. The passage begins with a series of commands, but in order to do these commands well—with a sincere, genuine attitude—we must have a belief that supports and informs them. That belief comes in verse 7: God cares for us.

USE THE SPECK METHOD TO STUDY 1 PETER 5:5-11 TO SEE HOW THIS BELIEF ALLOWS YOU TO HUMBLY ENCOURAGE AND SUPPORT OTHERS.

Marks Of A Disciple

A DISCIPLE'S HUMILITY GROWS WHEN THEIR *VALUE* COMES FROM GOD. (PSALM 139:13-16)

SINS TO AVOID

Make a list of any sins—wrong actions, attitudes, or thoughts—mentioned in the passage. These are the things to avoid in your life.

PROMISES TO CLAIM

Make a list of the promises in this passage. Promises give us confidence when we doubt God or face difficult times. So take them to heart and believe what they say.

EXAMPLES TO FOLLOW

What examples do you find in the passage? Is there a right way of thinking or acting described in the passage that you should take as an example for your life? Write it down.

COMMANDS TO OBEY

Write out all the commands you find. If a passage encourages you to take a certain action, take it as a command and write it down.

KNOWLEDGE OF GOD TO APPLY

What does the passage tell you about God that you can apply to your daily life? God's character shines throughout the Bible as an example for us.

DAY THREE
humility challenge

//

Have you ever heard little kids play the "My Daddy" game? "My daddy's so strong he can ..." "Well, my daddy's so strong he can ..." The game isn't really about their dads. It's about the children themselves. They want attention and respect.

This doesn't change as we get older. We want people to notice and think highly of us. And even though we move on from the "My Daddy" game, we still use conversation to accomplish this. We steer it toward topics we know more about or have experience in. When someone else tells a story, we find ways to top it. We don't allow others to finish their thoughts before we hijack the conversation with our own ideas, or we let our thoughts wander instead of actively listening to others.

On the other end of the spectrum, some people stay completely silent in conversations or avoid them completely. They hold in words that could encourage, help, or even connect with someone else. This leaves others feeling out on a limb or uncared for when they talk with this person. Are there times when you have something beneficial and helpful to say, but you choose to keep it inside? That's not humility; it's still self-focused—all about you and how you feel.

If we're honest, our conversations far too often increase our pride. But they don't have to; we can foster habits that grow humility instead. Look to Jesus as your example. Jesus mentioned his Father a lot, but he wasn't playing "My Daddy." He was genuinely focusing on God and on the relationship between God and the people he was talking with.

Here's a good rule to follow:

IF IT ISN'T HELPFUL OR ENCOURAGING, DON'T SAY IT.
IF IT IS, DON'T HOLD IT IN.

Choose one or two humility challenges to do in the next 24 hours, then write about the experience in the space provided at the end.

Go through an entire meal (with others!) without talking about yourself. Ask questions and follow-up questions, use encouragement, and listen well.

Have a conversation with someone you normally don't talk with. Ask at least five genuine questions.

Find two people to intentionally encourage today. Go beyond "good job" and "way to go," and tell them why you thought they did a good job.

Is there a person in your household you haven't had a real conversation with in a while? Find out how they are doing, and listen attentively to their answers.

Practice humble listening at school. Make eye contact with your teachers while they are speaking and with fellow students if you are working in a group. Listen when other students ask a question or make a comment in class.

What was hard about this?

What did you learn? Did anything surprise you?

DAY FOUR
stories

✗ ✗

Great stories have great heroes. As Christ-followers, we have the perfect hero and the ultimate storyteller writing our lives. Samuel Wells describes the story of the Christ-follower this way:

"Stories are told to [show off] the virtues of the hero—for if the hero failed, all would be lost. By contrast, a saint can fail in a way that the hero can't, because the failure of a saint reveals the forgiveness and the new possibilities made in God, and the saint is just a small character in a story that's always fundamentally about God."

Did you catch the last part of that quote? "The saint is just a small character in a story that's always fundamentally about God." This idea is the foundation of a humble walk with God. When we really believe the bigger story is about God and not us, we can be happy and content. We don't have to envy others' success or fame. Their roles in the story may seem bigger than ours, but in reality they're all small roles. The story is not about them either. We're all characters in a story that is really about God.

And because he is a good God, it's a good story. All the characters are significant. Each one has a particular role to play. When you step wholeheartedly into your role for the glory of God, you walk humbly with him.

TAKE A FEW MINUTES TODAY TO LOOK BACK OVER GOD'S STORY IN YOU OWN LIFE.

FOLLOW THE INSTRUCTIONS BELOW TO FILL OUT YOUR TIMELINE ON THE NEXT TWO PAGES.

1. MOUNTAINTOPS: First, identify the high points of your story—the moments that make you smile as you look back on them and that reflected your best. Make small mountains on the timeline and write down those moments.

2. VALLEYS: Next, identify the valleys or the low points of your story. These are the obstacles, hurts, trials, and mistakes. Draw some valleys in your timeline and fill in these moments.

3. TURNING POINTS: Every story has a turning point, a moment when everything changes and the plot thickens. Identify the turning points in your own story with a circular arrow and mark down what the turning point was for you.

4. CHARACTERS: Other characters play a vital role in our story. Look at your mountains, valleys, and turning points, and write down the names of people who played a role in each of these places.

5. THE AUTHOR: Now take a minute to look at the story of your life. Think back to Samuel Wells's wisdom about how our stories (the highpoints and the low points) are really made to reflect the hero and author of a greater story. Use a different color pen to identify God's fingerprints in your story. How was he involved in the high points and what do they say about him? How was he at work in the low points? Was he there? What was he thinking or feeling during those times? And last, what role did God play in the turning points? How did he show up when the plot thickened?

MY TIMELINE

HEBREWS SAYS THAT GOD IS THE AUTHOR AND PERFECTER OF OUR FAITH. WHEN WE START TO LOOK AT OUR LIVES IN LIGHT OF HIS GREATER STORY, OUR PERSPECTIVE CHANGES. OUR WALK WITH HIM GETS CLOSER, AND OUR HUMILITY GIVES US FREEDOM TO RISK, MAKE MISTAKES, AND BE A PART OF THE GREATEST STORY EVER TOLD.

DAY FIVE
invited

//

Sometimes we think that being humble means becoming a doormat—constantly putting ourselves down and allowing others to walk all over us. Other times, we confuse being humble with being invisible, and we attempt to be small and unnoticed

But in doing this, we rob God of glory. God has given each of us special gifts and abilities, and he wants us to use them. By being the people God made us to be, we glorify him. We see a picture of this in Romans 15. Paul writes about everything he's done to tell people about Jesus—the signs and wonders and his missionary journeys.

If Paul translated humility as being a doormat or invisible, we wouldn't have Romans 15 and we wouldn't know about the miracles God did. With true humility, Paul told the whole story. He didn't avoid talking about these things or minimize his contribution. But he also didn't claim the glory for himself. He gave it all to God. "God gave the duty; I simply proclaimed," he said. "I shared the gospel; God changed the listeners' hearts."

Paul recognized that the great work was God's, and that God had given him the privilege of being involved.

READ ROMANS 15:14-20 AND USE THE 5P METHOD TO STUDY THIS PASSAGE OF SCRIPTURE.

PURPOSE Why do you think the author wrote this? Why is it important enough to be in the Bible? In a sentence or two, write what you think the overall theme or topic is.

>>

PRIMARY VERSE Which verse or phrase stands out to you the most? What do you think is catching your attention?

>>

PROMISES List any promises you find. You may need to think deeply about this one because promises are sometimes inferred or implied.

>>

PROBLEMS If you read something here that doesn't make sense to you—a word, a phrase, an idea—write it down as a question. Then search for the answer by asking someone who might understand the Bible a bit better.

>>

PRACTICAL APPLICATION Think about how this passage might actually change your life. What needs to be different in how you live, think, and feel? Be specific—your application should tell who, what, and when.

>>

DAY SIX
walking with God

Have you ever thought about what it really takes to have a best friend? Think about how many hours you and your best friend have spent together. Or how many conversations you've had in person or over texts. Best friends help us make lots of decisions, from hairstyles to college applications. And they have access to parts of our lives that few others do, like what we're really like after drinking too much caffeine during a late-night Netflix marathon, or what we sound like singing along to the radio. So it's no surprise that the more you hang out with your best friends, the more you become like them. You start finishing each other's sentences, using the same expressions, and even sharing some of the same mannerisms.

It's the same way with God. When we do life with him, we start to pick up some of his traits. It's as if we know him well enough to finish his sentences. When we walk with God daily, we look for his input in our decisions, let him into the corners of our lives (no matter how dusty they are), and miss him terribly when we don't connect with him.

Micah tells us to walk humbly with God, and today we're going to focus on the *walk* part of that verse. It's been said that to be much *like* Christ, we should be much *with* Christ. Consider how you can walk with Christ like you walk through life with your best friend. Then try out one of these challenges today.

1. INVITE GOD INTO A MAJOR DECISION. If you are facing a big decision in your life, take 10 minutes today and invite God into it. Find a distraction-free place and tell God about this decision—your worries or why the decision is so hard to make. Lay it out for God in the first five minutes, and then spend the next five minutes listening to him. Ask what he thinks and quietly connect with him. You may find an answer, reassurance, or some peace. But you definitely will find connection with the God who holds your entire life in his hands.

2. IF YOU'RE LIKE MOST PEOPLE, there are some parts of your life that not many others have seen: fears, struggles, and temptations. Spend 10 minutes today letting God help you sweep out those dusty corners. Tell God everything, ask for help, and confess anything you need to.

3. WHAT DOES GOD THINK OF YOU? If you had to make a list of what your best friend thinks of you, it would probably be pretty easy. So today, make a list of what God thinks of you. Dig around the Bible for verses that tell you his thoughts about his children. And when you're finished, consider how these verses affect your relationship with him.

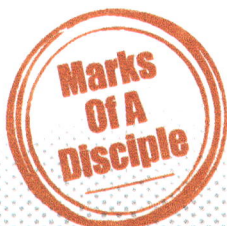

Marks Of A Disciple

A DISCIPLE *WALKS HUMBLY* WITH GOD. (GENESIS 6:9)

DAY SEVEN
rest

//.

You know the routine. Take today off from this journal and use it to connect with God. Consider changing it up a bit: connect with God by praying as you take a walk. Get together with a good friend or mentor and tell them how you're growing in your faith or what God has been teaching you (and visa versa). Memorize a verse of Scripture or find some time and space to just be still with God. However you spend your time today, focus it on connecting with God.

FINALLY, BROTHERS, WHATEVER IS TRUE, WHATEVER IS NOBLE, WHATEVER IS RIGHT, WHATEVER IS PURE, WHATEVER IS LOVELY, WHATEVER IS ADMIRABLE – IF ANYTHING IS EXCELLENT OR PRAISEWORTHY – THINK ABOUT SUCH THINGS.

-

PHILIPPIANS 4:8

WEEK FOUR

know Jesus

DAY ONE *intro*

x x x x x x x x x x x x x x x x x x x x x x x x x x x

**HE HAS SHOWED YOU, O MAN, WHAT IS GOOD. AND WHAT DOES THE LORD REQUIRE OF YOU? TO *ACT JUSTLY* AND TO *LOVE MERCY* AND TO *WALK HUMBLY WITH YOUR GOD.*
MICAH 6:8**

The best example of someone living out the commands in Micah 6:8 is (you guessed it) Jesus. Acting with justice, loving mercy, and walking humbly with God—these are all practices Jesus did on a consistent basis. So when it comes to following Jesus as our savior and guide, we need to find ways to practice these things too. We can't do it on our own; we need Christ to transform our hearts from the inside out in order to live the way he wants us to live. If we try to do it on our own, we will end up like the Pharisees, hypocrites with exteriors that look good, but interiors that are hollow and cold.

This week take time to explore what it means to follow Jesus with Micah 6:8 as your guide. Use this journal to write down your experiences, to process your thoughts and feelings, and to record what God does in and through you. Invite Christ to transform your heart, but be ready—when he does, nothing will ever be the same again!

DAY ONE
inside out

//

Have you ever put on a piece of clothing inside out, but didn't realize it? Little kids do this all the time—they wear their shirt backwards, have their socks on inside out, or wear shoes on the wrong feet. They need someone to point out their mistake to get things back to how they were intended. The same is true of following Jesus: he wants to turn our inside-out lives back the way they were intended. We may think we are doing all the right religious stuff—attending church, reading the Bible, praying regularly, going on mission trips—but if we're doing them because of a checklist mentality rather than a heart transformation, we're missing the whole point.

This is the problem God was using Micah to address in the Old Testament. People had turned their faith into a checklist of sacrifices that placed a higher value on rituals than on relationship with God. Now that's inside out! Micah 6:8 corrects this system by asking for lives lived out of a heart connection with God, not a checklist of good things to do. Jesus tells us to live the same way.

SPEND SOME TIME TODAY ANSWERING THESE QUESTIONS AND IDENTIFYING HOW JESUS MIGHT BE FIXING YOUR INSIDE-OUT LIFE THIS WEEK. INVITE HIM TO TRANSFORM YOUR HEART!

Fill in the left column below with a list of all the "religious" activities and habits you have in your life, from attending church to prayer to Bible study—anything you can think of. Next to each activity, in the right column, write down why you do it. Be honest!

WHAT DO YOU DO?

WHY DO YOU DO IT?

Who is someone in your life who seems to live authentically and honestly? How can you tell?

If you could instantly change one character flaw or bad habit in your life, what would you choose? Why?

Why do you think God seems more interested in our hearts than our behaviors?

DAY TWO
legalism or grace

Let's be honest: following Jesus by acting justly, loving mercy, and walking humbly with God sounds really great, but it can be pretty difficult to practice in everyday life. Thankfully, we're not alone in this. The book of Romans is a letter the apostle Paul wrote to the church in Rome, which was made up of both Jews and Gentiles (non-Jews). They were struggling to understand and live out the gospel of Jesus as a very diverse group of people. Jews didn't normally hang out with Gentiles, and vice versa. So when the gospel brought them together in one church, they had to figure out what this new spiritual movement would look like. Sometimes people slipped into legalism, trying really hard to be good people without relationship with Jesus behind their actions. That's why Paul gives them an encouragement in Romans: it's all about grace!

READ ROMANS 9:30–32. CHOOSE ONE OF THE BIBLE STUDY METHODS OUT OF THE THREE YOU'VE BEEN USING OVER THE LAST FEW WEEKS.

5P (PAGE 8)
SPECK (PAGE 16)
OPA (PAGE 28)

DISCIPLES OF CHRIST KNOW THAT GOD'S *GRACE* IS SUFFICIENT. (2 CORINTHIANS 12:9)

DAY THREE
verbs

//

When we read Micah 6:8, it's full of verbs: Act. Love. Walk. (I'm sure you've caught that by now!) It implies that we have to *do* something, to *practice* justice and mercy and humility. When Jesus confronted the Pharisees (the hypocrites) and called them to do the same, he was addressing their heart condition. But he was also inviting them into practical action—when their hearts were changed, their behaviors and habits should change too.

TODAY, DO ONE OF THE FOLLOWING CHALLENGES IN ORDER TO PRACTICE JUSTICE, MERCY, AND HUMILITY IN THE NAME OF JESUS. STRETCH YOURSELF! THEN WRITE DOWN YOUR THOUGHTS AND FEELINGS ABOUT THE EXPERIENCE.

>> We all know a moocher or a freeloader—someone who owes us. Forgive their debt, big or small, and forget about it. Don't even bring it up to them; just show them mercy and forgive them.

>> Go this entire week without verbally whining or complaining (Phil. 2:14), even if someone is being annoying or a situation is frustrating. Redirect your thoughts by thanking God in that moment for who he is and what he's done, remembering that he has shown you mercy for your annoying habits too.

It's easy to become skeptical of beggars on street corners. This week, don't debate whether or not you should give. Just give. Keep a gift card to a restaurant in your car or backpack so you can give it away.

Spread some justice by choosing to stand up for someone who is being picked on. Help end injustice by choosing not to make fun of anyone this week.

What was hard about this?

What did you learn?

Did anything surprise you?

DAY FOUR
unconditional

✕ ✕

What is the point of going to church? Have you ever thought about that? Maybe you've gone because it's what good Christians do, or your parents made you, or you've just sort of always done it. The same goes with reading the Bible: why do we do this? To find ways to be good people? Maybe. But we can totally attend church and read the Bible without ever becoming a true Christ-follower or putting our faith and trust in Jesus.

We aren't followers of Christ because we follow rules. We're followers of Christ because of love. The difference between legalism and following Christ is striking: legalism says that I do good works in order to gain God's love and favor. Following Christ says I have already gained God's love and favor in Jesus, so I am now free and empowered to do good works. In both cases, we should be doing good things, but they are done for completely different reasons. God's love in Christ is unconditional—he's not going to love you more or less based on your behavior, good or bad! He doesn't need your good works; he wants your heart.

"LEGALISM IS SELF-RIGHTEOUSNESS. IT IS THE BELIEF THAT GOD IS SATISFIED WITH OUR ATTEMPT TO OBEY A MORAL CODE."

-ERWIN W. LUTZER

TAKE A FEW MINUTES TO MULL OVER HOW GOD'S UNCONDITIONAL LOVE AFFECTS YOUR LIFE BY ANSWERING THE FOLLOWING QUESTIONS.

How would you describe *legalism* in your own words? What comes to mind when you hear the word *legalism*?

Why is it so difficult for people to believe in the unconditional love of God?

In your own words, write down what makes someone a Christ-follower.

Do you think Christ wants our actions to change? Why or why not?

DAY FIVE
missing the point

//

If you ever find yourself in the unfortunate situation of standing in front of a judge in a courtroom for a crime you've committed, the word *stressful* would probably describe your day. Whether the infraction is minor or serious, being in a courtroom situation is scary because you're being judged by your actions.

When Paul writes about being "justified" in the Bible, he's bringing up the image of a courtroom. For those who practice legalism and religious duty, it's as if they're standing before God the Judge and saying, "Check out all the awesome religious and morally upright things I've done! You've gotta love me now!" They put their faith in their own ability to keep all the laws set up in the Old Testament.

But they're misunderstanding God's nature and love. He doesn't love us for what we do, but for who we are in Christ. He invites us to live, not by our own moral strength, but by our faith in his strength for us. As you read the words of Paul in Galatians, remember the courtroom. Christ stood in our place and offered us new life in him!

READ GALATIANS 2:15-21 AND USE THE OPA STUDY METHOD.

OBSERVATION

Compile all the facts found in these passages. Make 20 to 30 observations about what you read.

PRINCIPLES

Draw a few principles from the observations you made. What is God trying to teach you in this passage?

APPLICATION

How will you apply these principles to your life? Be specific—a good application will tell who, what, and when.

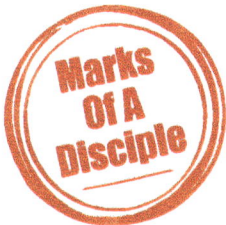

Marks Of A Disciple

DISCIPLES KNOW THEY ARE *JUSTIFIED* BY CHRIST, NOT BY WHAT THEY DO. (ROMANS 5:1)

DAY SIX
listening

We live in a culture of noise and doing. We like to be on the go, we fill our calendars with activity, and we get uncomfortable if we sit in silence for too long. Think about it: when you have nothing to do for even a few seconds, don't you feel tempted to check your phone or tap your foot, just something to keep your mind occupied? Living inside out (remember Day 1 of this week) and planting our faith in our heart instead of our actions sometimes means removing distractions from our lives. When it comes to practicing justice and mercy, we have to rely on Christ's strength to work in and through us. And that means choosing to stop the busyness to listen for God's voice to guide you.

TODAY, SPEND 30 MINUTES ALONE IN SILENT PRAYER. NO MUSIC OR TV OR COMPUTER OR PHONE OR ANYONE ELSE. NOT EVEN A JOURNAL. JUST YOU AND GOD.

First, find a location where you can be completely alone and undistracted. In the Sermon on the Mount, Jesus encouraged his followers to go pray in their closets. Try that! Maybe you'd prefer to be outside in nature or in a room in your church.

When you get to that quiet location, close your eyes, be still and quiet, and just listen for God. You'll probably find your mind wandering and getting distracted. That's okay; notice what comes to the surface in your mind and ask God why you're thinking about that right now. Just breathe in and out. If you find yourself getting too distracted, focus on a word from our study this week: *mercy*. Repeat it a few times in your mind and heart until you can refocus on listening to God.

Jesus did all sorts of amazing acts of justice and mercy through his intimate relationship with the Father. He developed that relationship through prayer and alone times with God. This is where justice and mercy begin, not with our own efforts and activities, but in silence before God. Listen! He is speaking, and he will guide you.

When you've done this challenge, write down what you heard from God, if anything, and what your experience was like.

"VERY EARLY IN THE MORNING, WHILE IT WAS STILL DARK, JESUS GOT UP, LEFT THE HOUSE AND WENT OFF TO A SOLITARY PLACE, WHERE HE PRAYED." –MARK 1:35

DAY SEVEN
the end ... for now

You know the drill by now. Today is your day off! It's also the last day of this entire study.

CONGRATULATIONS!

NOTES: Quotations taken from THE COMPLETE GATHERED GOLD, A treasury of quotations for Christians, John Blanchard, ed. Evangelical Press, 2006.

While you may not have any more questions to answer or challenges to complete, your walk with God has many more incredible miles left. This journal was designed to give you some of the tools you need to keep going down the road with God.

There used to be a famous Nike poster featuring a picture of a runner. Under the picture it read, "There is no finish line." The message of the poster was clear—while there are many races in life, the committed are in it for the long haul. They live life to the fullest and embrace the adventure instead of thinking only about when they'll be done.

Walking closely with God is the riskiest adventure you can join. Anything can happen. He holds a map that will lead you into territory you've never even dreamed of. And your job? Stick close to him. Don't let go, not for a second.

JOIN GOD'S ADVENTURE FOR YOUR LIFE AND LIVE WITHOUT A FINISH LINE.